IN THE MIDST OF CHAOS, PEACE

IN
THE
MIDST
OF
CHAOS,
PEACE

COMPILED AND EDITED BY
Daniel Thomas Paulos

WITH REFLECTIONS BY
Sister Wendy Beckett

AND SILHOUETTE PAPER-CUTS BY
Sister Mary Jean Dorcy, O.P.
(1914–1988)
AND
Daniel Thomas Paulos

IGNATIUS PRESS
San Francisco

The author wishes to acknowledge:
Sister Wendy Beckett and the Dominican Sisters of Edmonds for contributing their royalties to St. Bernadette Institute of Sacred Art; Carlyn Iuzzolino for her initial editing; and the publishers of the following books from which Sister Wendy's reflections were adapted: Harper San Francisco, *The Gaze of Love* and *The Mystery of Love*; Dorling Kindersley Publishing, New York, *Sister Wendy's Book of Saints*; *Joy; Love; Peace*, and *Silence*; Stewart, Tabori and Chang, New York, *Sister Wendy's Grand Tour*. All reflections are solely owned by Sister Wendy Beckett and are used with her permission and blessings.

Cover art by Daniel Thomas Paulos
Cover photograph of Sister Wendy by Margaret Young
Cover design by Riz Boncan Marsella

Royalties from this book support the works of
St. Bernadette Institute of Sacred Art
P.O. Box 8249, Albuquerque, NM 87198

FIRST PRINTING
Published by Ignatius Press, San Francisco
ISBN: 0–89870–752–8
Library of Congress catalogue number: 99–73018
Printed in the United States of America ∞

PREFACE

Nothing matters but God. This is another way of saying that everything matters. God is not "out there" or even "in here". God is everywhere and comes to us in every experience and emotion. It is for us to recognize His presence, whether in pain—a Crucified Presence—or in joy—a Risen Presence—or in the ordinary—a Nazareth Presence. There is no black-and-white with God, merely the overwhelmingness of His immediacy.

It is precisely because this immediacy is so hard to grasp, so beyond our natural capacity, that we need images such as these delicate papercuts to spell out for us these essentials.

Sister Mary Jean Dorcy and Dan Paulos extract the essence of the Gospel message and outline it with the most exquisite finesse. They are using a form of visual equivalence, translating what is complex and overpowering into what is simple and understandable.

This is the art of the parable, far more profound than it may seem. The more humbly we contemplate these works in which the scissors and blade have replaced the brush but are used with the same artistic skill, the more we shall come to understand the absoluteness of our God.

SISTER WENDY BECKETT

FOREWORD

At first glance, the three collaborators of this book may seem to be an unlikely alliance, as they represent three different generations from very different backgrounds. The late Sister Jean Dorcy, O.P., of Irish ancestry, was born in the state of Washington in 1914. Sister Wendy Beckett is a native of South Africa who now lives in England and is a member of the generation born between the two World Wars. Daniel Thomas Paulos, an artist of Italian-Greek-Norwegian heritage who was raised in Iowa and now lives in New Mexico, belongs to the "baby-boom" generation.

The traits that unite these three people, however, will become immediately apparent even to the casual reader of this volume. Each collaborator sees the medium of art as a means of praising the grandeur of God and illustrating the endless variety of gifts the Creator has showered upon mankind. For them, art is prayer, and all of their work reflects that deep spirituality. The three collaborators also share the common experience of accidentally falling into the medium that made them famous. Indeed, their many admirers likely feel that the hand of God is apparent in the events that shaped the lives of Sister Jean, Sister Wendy, and Dan Paulos.

Until her death in 1988, Sister Jean Dorcy was one of the most famous papercutting artists in the world. She was best known for her religious silhouettes, though children were also a favorite topic. She eventually produced thousands of cuttings and authored twenty-six books—many for children—most of which were illustrated by her own graceful, airy, black-and-white silhouettes. But Sister Jean's career had an inauspicious beginning.

Baptized Frances Emma Dorcy, Sister Jean was the youngest of nine children. She entered the novitiate of the Dominican Sisters of the Holy Cross in 1932, at the age of eighteen, choosing the religious name Sister Mary Jean. However, the young novice had difficulty finding her niche in the convent, seeming to have no talent for either nursing or teaching. One day, the mistress of novices handed Sister Jean a framed cut-paper silhouette from Austria and asked her to copy it. Though she had little experience with papercutting—other than cutting out pictures from the Sears catalog as a child—Sister

Jean succeeded in producing a papercutting just like the one she had been given, thus launching her artistic career. As her talent blossomed, Sister Jean favored as her subject matter the images dearest to her heart: religious figures and the orphaned children for whom she cared. It is no accident that her best-known silhouettes depict the Infant Jesus and His Blessed Mother, for Sister Jean considered the Madonna and Child to be "inseparables". Some of the silhouettes created by Sister Jean have found their way into art collections and museums around the world, including the permanent collection of the Smithsonian Institution in Washington, D.C. Other cuttings are held as precious treasures by individuals or organizations to whom Sister Jean made a gift of her work in return for a kindness extended to her.

Sister Jean's cuttings that appear in this volume have not been shared previously with a wide audience. Some of her silhouettes are from a collection of original cuttings that supposedly was destroyed when a publisher who was going out of business burned an inventory he thought to be worthless. The cuttings were considered lost until Sister Jean's agent, Dan Paulos, later discovered them in a Chicago friary. Since some of the negatives of Sister Jean's work are old and inferior in quality to today's photographic materials, the reader should keep in mind that the original cuttings on black paper produced a clearer, sharper image than those depicted in some of the photographs of her silhouettes in this collection.

Like Sister Jean, Wendy Beckett felt a call to religious life as a teenager. In 1946, when she was sixteen, Wendy left South Africa to enter the Sisters of Notre Dame in Great Britain, where she had lived as a child. After obtaining a degree in English literature from St. Anne's College at Oxford, Sister Wendy returned to South Africa, where she taught until 1970, when health problems forced her to retire from teaching.

Sister Wendy moved back to England and received permission from the Vatican to live a semi-contemplative life as a consecrated virgin. She settled into a small trailer on the grounds of the Carmelite convent in Norfolk, England, where she could lead a life of solitude, prayer, and poverty under the protection of the Carmelites. Even though she spent most of her day in prayer, Sister Wendy found time to indulge a lifelong interest in art, and she regularly borrowed art books from the public library mobile van that occasionally visited the convent area. In the early 1980s, she began to write articles for art journals in order to contribute some financial assistance to the Carmelite sisters who were supporting her.

Then a divine accident occurred. Sister Wendy was attending an art exhibit in Norfolk in the late 1980s when a television producer who was in the gallery on another assignment overheard her talking with her friend about a painting. He was so impressed with Sister Wendy's lively commentary on the painting that he asked permission to film her. Following this, a BBC executive happened to see the videotape of Sister Wendy on a local television channel, and the rest is, as they say, history.

Now known worldwide as the "Art Nun", Sister Wendy has hosted a number of art programs for the BBC, and her ten-part art series broadcast on PBS stations in the United States has been a big hit. Yet, Sister Wendy seems rather bemused by a fame that she never invited, and she has remained focused on her life of prayer and consecration to Almighty God. The deep and refreshing spiritual perspective of Sister Wendy, which often is ignored by the popular media, is reflected in her meditations chosen by Dan Paulos for this volume.

Daniel Thomas Paulos was raised in Sioux City, Iowa, one of eight children. The greatest joy of his days in Catholic grade school was spending time with his teachers, the Sisters of Christian Charity, who modeled a heavenly reverence for the God they served and an earthly compassion for poor and suffering people. Consequently, when one of the sisters asked twelve-year-old Dan Paulos to re-create some Dorcy silhouettes for the school bulletin board, the youngster tried so hard to please her that he cut his fingers with a double-edged razor blade trying to get the cutting just right.

Nevertheless, that bloody experience hooked the young Paulos on the work of Sister Jean Dorcy. He wrote her a fan letter, and, to the surprise of his teachers, the famous artist answered by return mail, enclosing some samples of her cuttings. Paulos continued to correspond with Sister Jean and eventually met her in 1969 in Albuquerque, New Mexico, where she was recuperating from lung surgery and he had joined the Brothers of the Good Shepherd.

After ten years in religious life, Dan Paulos decided that his real vocation was in the world, and he has been expressing his deep religious faith through his art ever since. An accomplished calligrapher, sculptor, and painter, Paulos worked on his own art as he deepened his friendship with Sister Jean. She encouraged him to employ his own artistic skills in the papercutting medium, but initially Paulos was too timid to cut his sketches. Instead, he painted his first silhouettes with black and white acrylics. Sister Jean eventually convinced him to cut the images he had sketched, and she tutored him along the way, even as she battled lung problems and arthritis that crippled her hands so badly that she had to discontinue her own cutting. Paulos became Sister Jean's student, friend, and confidant during her twenty years of convalescence, making regular trips to visit her after she returned to Seattle.

Under Sister Jean's tutelage, Paulos built his skills as a serious and talented paper-cutter, developing his own unique style, which Sister Jean described in this way: "Where my cuttings have a fanciful lightness of touch, Dan's are strong and forceful, taking a free and independent form." After he had proven himself a master of the papercutting medium, Paulos received the ultimate compliment when Sister Jean asked him to cut some of the designs she had sketched but was unable to cut because of her arthritic hands. The two artists working together thus became a productive team, creating ap-proximately twenty finished silhouettes together. Dan Paulos went on to become Sister Jean's agent, spending two or three weeks a year with her in Seattle, even as he pursued his own career as a serious papercutter.

Paulos has developed a considerable reputation for his designs rendered in his papercuttings. Like his mentor, Sister Jean, he has become one of the most famous papercutting artists of the twentieth century, with his work hanging in collections and galleries around the world. Paulos has produced compelling cut-paper silhouettes de-picting his compassion for suffering humanity, but he is best known for his Madonnas, which reflect his deep devotion to the Blessed Mother.

In spite of his own artistic accomplishments, Dan Paulos has never forgotten the influence of Sister Jean Dorcy, whom he continues to describe as his best friend, even ten years after her death. Paulos helped showcase her work in the book *Spring Comes to the Hill Country*, a collection of Sister Jean's silhouettes, illustrated by his calligraphy. His tribute to Sister Jean continues in this volume, which presents the work of both the famous teacher and her accomplished student.

Always a great admirer of women religious, Dan Paulos has published two other books focused on sisters: *He's Put the Whole World in Her Hands*, a collection of quotes from Mother Teresa of Calcutta, illustrated by his art; and *Behold the Women*, a collection of various essays, poems, photographs, and paintings that offer tribute to women reli-gious. It was only natural, then, that Paulos was attracted to the writings of the "Art Nun". For this book, he obtained Sister Wendy's permission to include selections from her writings that particularly touched his own heart and soul. While each verse and each silhouette is a meditation in itself, some of the verses reflect the silhouettes they accompany. Other verses are not related to the silhouettes in any way, except that all the selections in this book offer glory to God.

Readers, therefore, will delight in picking up this volume for a few moments of meditation and prayer or for several hours of joyful contemplation. Indeed, the three individuals who are brought together on these pages, no doubt by divine accident, have created a little touch of heavenly peace that will be savored for years to come.

ANN CAREY

Writer
South Bend, Indiana

PAPERCUTTING: THE FOLK ART OF THE WORLD

Papercutting could well be called the folk art of the world. Just about every culture around the globe developed a tradition of designs or images cut from paper or paper-like material soon after the material became available. The art form, which naturally developed as a folk art or craft, appeared in various places over a period of many centuries. Rather than spreading from continent to continent, however, it seems to have developed independently over and over, although there are a few obvious cases of the concept being borrowed from one population by another.

From ancient Egypt to ancient China and to all of Asia, across India's varied cultures, and throughout the Jewish and Turkic groups of the Middle East, papercutting has been practiced and even revered. And, throughout Europe and the New World, cut-paper work has been spread by immigrants and reinvented any number of times to serve endless purposes. Some traditions of papercutting have endowed the creations with spiritual importance (as in pre-conquest Mexico); others have bent the art form to spiritual or religious uses (as in Roman Catholic monasteries of late medieval Europe), without making the art work in itself sacred. Indeed, it would be easier to list the indigenous cultures where cut-work never developed or took root than those where papercutting flourished at one time or another.

It even seems that cut-paper work developed, before contact with Europe, in the Hawaiian Islands, where kapa or tapa "cloth" was sometimes embellished with cut-work. After contact with Europe, Hawaiian papercutting was used primarily to create intricate quilting patterns.

EARLY PAPERCUTTERS

Egyptian papyrus in sheets or rolls was not well-suited to being decorated with cut-outs, and yet some papyri had spaces between the painted figures cut away. Cut-outs made the work more interesting, perhaps more beautiful, but much less strong and more likely to be destroyed, even with careful handling. Cut-outs in leather were not so destabilizing, so cut work grew to higher levels of elaboration in areas where the flat, pre-paper material available was animal skins, often pounded to near transparency. In some Asian-Pacific cultures these cut-outs from pounded hides became, over time, the basic figures of the shadow theater—both secular and religious—and many have survived for centuries.

When pulp-based papermaking was developed in China—at least two thousand years ago—the art of papercutting evolved right alongside the paper. Cloth cut-outs both for appliqué and as embroidery guides were already common. At first, paper merely made the work of making patterns and guides a little easier. Soon, however, the papercuttings were being made for themselves, for their beauty and their capacity to decorate, instruct, or inspire. Figures of gods and amulets of luck cut from paper have been found in good condition (meaning they were at least sometimes intentionally preserved) in archeological digs in China dating back to 150 B.C.

The Arabian conquest of Samarkand in A.D. 750 became a landmark in world history, in the history of the evolution of papermaking, and, naturally enough, in the history of papercutting. The Arab conquerors of Samarkand discovered a well-developed paper industry that included a healthy export business of paper going to the East. They simply added westward trade routes, by way of which the Middle East and the Mediterranean came into possession of paper.

There is no evidence that papercutting was transmitted along with the paper and the secrets of papermaking, but, like many others, the Jewish people of the Eastern Mediterranean began using the new material for documents. They developed a tradition that continues to this day of decorating important documents with calligraphy, ornamental ink, and paint and with papercutting. Wedding contracts, called *ketubahs*, and symbolic images of New Jerusalem so decorated are among the most highly treasured antique keepsakes in some Jewish families and among collectors of pre-modern Judaica. An ordinary Jewish home a thousand years ago would commonly have had a Mizrah on the wall, an indicator of the direction to Jerusalem, the direction to turn to in prayer. Many of the better examples of this practical, religious art were at least partly accomplished by papercutting. Jewish papercutting was a nearly lost art by the nineteenth century, but in our time it is flourishing again, thanks largely to the efforts of Yaakov Neeman and Yehudit Shadur.

The Moors—Arabs of northwestern Africa who conquered Spain and became a great influence in civilized Europe in the eighth century—were great devotees of learning and libraries, so they brought papermaking with them. For nearly seven hundred years, the Moors remained in Europe, and their reverence for learning, paper, and elaborate art forms became a permanent part of the cultural matrix of the continent. The Moors were Moslems, and there were papercutters among the Moslems, but not many. In fact, Arab papercutting has never been a very developed art form, perhaps owing to the prohibition on organic forms or "graven images" in Arab art. However, both the Jews of the Eastern Mediterranean and later Eastern Europe and the Roman Catholics in the remainder of Mediterranean Europe developed finer forms of papercutting once they had access to the material—thanks to Arab movements in war and conquest.

In our time some very fine Moslem cut-paper work is being done, but not in the Arabian areas. The few Islamic papercutters known live in India and eastern Turkey. Actually, Turkey is the home of another very old tradition of cut-paper work, which, although seldom religious in nature, could be called Islamic art in view of the fact that the artists were almost certainly Moslems. The oldest Turkish cut-paper work, however, seems to have been done more to glorify various exalted rulers than to celebrate a relationship with God.

By the time the Renaissance was reestablishing the appreciation of art and beauty in the cultures of Europe, the religious orders and devout hermits of the late Middle Ages were already (or, perhaps, still) practicing the ornamental arts in their copying of sacred texts, their records of the Church, and, sometimes, in the form of art to be sold or given to patrons. Like the Jewish tradition of papercutting, the Roman Catholic applications of the art form were eclipsed in recent centuries by developing technologies of art, print, and decoration.

Recent centuries of papercutting

The fate of cut-paper work around the world was endangered by many forces, particularly the "rush" over the past several centuries to embrace what is new. The availability of brightly colored paints, for instance, made the intricate, colorful papercuttings of Poland and Eastern Europe somehow less important. After all, if multiple layers of paper were cut and pierced to create a decorative pattern to be applied to a wall or chair or window, it would probably have to be done again next year to replace the worn cutting. But if the same decoration were done with paints, it could merely be touched up. Paint, printing technology, cheaper inks, better pens, and, eventually, the development of the camera all contributed in a variety of ways to the decline of papercutting from the late Renaissance to the nineteenth century.

Even the *Klosterarbeit*, or art work of the cloistered orders in Europe, faded away to a large extent in this period, largely a result of the same influences. Prayer cards and title pages that might have been the work of days or weeks could be made—some thought no less nobly—in short order using more modern techniques.

Nonetheless, papercutting survived as a result of at least two influences: poverty and pleasure. The poorest among us can never afford what is newest. When cameras and photographers, for example, were rare and expensive, it became fashionable to have photographic portraits of family members made and to display them prominently. These photographs were replacing the even more expensive paintings that had been fashionable before them. But the poor, struggling to survive in many cases, also struggled to have what was fashionable: portraits of loved ones. Artists who did not master the intricacies of color had, in some times and places, mastered instead the outline or silhouette. A painted silhouette could be had cheaply, decorated with intricate ornamentation, and serve nicely as the "needed" portrait. By the eighteenth century, an even cheaper and often better silhouette portrait was commonly available in the form of cut-paper. Some of the papercutting portraitists became world famous and traveled from continent to continent, frequently stopping in smaller towns and villages, while painters and later photographers stopped only in the larger cities, where money was more plentiful.

Poverty also kept some of the decorative uses of papercutting active in Eastern Europe and remote parts of Turkey, while tradition itself—aided by poverty—kept papercutting alive in China and helped it spread to other parts of Asia.

If poverty had been the only influence ensuring the life of cut-paper work, it would not have survived into the twentieth century at all. The other techniques and technologies of art and reproduction, following the usual course of inventions, became accessible to ordinary people, even to the very poor. The other force at work was a nobler one: the pleasure taken in papercutting itself by both the artists and the afficionados.

Papercutting allows the artist to leave more room for the viewers' imagination than most modern art forms do. The shadow suggests more but leaves more to be guessed at. The outline indicates a great deal but does not demand that every viewer fill in the spaces the same way. The special pleasure provided by an art form that gives less information and encourages more imagination fits papercutting perfectly for art that would do certain tasks.

Art as amusement, for example, has developed in only two major forms: the caricature and the silhouette portrait. They thrive side by side throughout the world wherever people congregate in sufficient numbers to support the artists. So silhouettes of cut-paper from amusement parks and boardwalks share wall space in modern homes with similar silhouettes that may date back centuries.

Art as illustration is another area where the silhouette or cut-paper image has a power not easily matched by more "finished" and detailed art forms. Children especially like the freedom of imagination allowed when their books are illustrated completely or partially in silhouette. Devotional art is also an area where too much detail can be an intrusion of sorts. How like the viewer is the saint? How accessible is our Lady? Often, the silhouette illustration—painted or cut from paper—is the one into which the viewer is best able to project his needs and lose his sorrows because it does not demand that the holy figure be this color or have these details or those. So silhouette images of the saints and the Blessed Virgin have been created, appreciated, and collected in Europe and the New World for centuries. In certain eras they were more common than in others, but they represent a tradition never completely lost.

Art as tradition, too, calls the papercutter to the fore. There is a sense of history in the activity of papercutting that is easily grasped, often even turning the papercutter into a performing artist. The simplicity of the cut-paper craft allows the artist to exercise his higher expressive intentions—the art—in a style that is easily accessible to most viewers, while giving all concerned a sense of connectedness with a continuing and longstanding tradition.

Papercutting in our time

The twentieth century has been a time of paradoxes for papercutting. Displaced in the pedestrian arts by cameras and electronic media, papercutting has been taken up by fine artists and has given them tremendous power to express themselves in unimagined ways. The founders of what we call modern art often started their careers as papercutters and collagists. Georges Braque and Yves Saint Laurent did some of the dramatic work that launched their careers in cut-paper. Henri Matisse favored cut-paper both early in his artistic life and toward the end, when his eyesight and the limits of his aging body made painting difficult or impossible for him.

By the middle of the twentieth century, papercutters everywhere thought of themselves as lone representatives of a lost art form. Magazine articles about papercutters frequently praised the one artist known to the writer as the "last" of a long and honored line of artists in a lost art form. One article in *Life* magazine, featuring the work of Walter von Gunten, a Swiss-German papercutter living and working in the U.S. since the 1960s, attributed the papercuttings to an unidentified master of the form, probably Austrian and dead for a century or so. Some years later, an airline magazine appropriated another of von Gunten's papercuttings, again assuming that such work was not done in our century. Mr. von Gunten lived to laugh at and correct both publications.

In the Netherlands and later in other countries, papercutters began to discover one another and to form guilds and clubs of various kinds. Urged by these groups, museums have devoted whole shows to both historic and contemporary papercutting throughout Europe and the U.S. Old collections are being given new attention, and artists and crafters currently working in cut-paper have been attracting attention that had not been given to papercutting over the previous fifty or more years.

Most twentieth-century papercutting has been purely decorative. The work of the great innovators of fine art—Matisse et al.—has been a very small part of the cut-paper work of our time. The excellent cut-paper book illustrations of such masters as Holden Wetherbee and Ugo Mochi have been far from common. And the arresting work of Sister Mary Jean Dorcy and Dan Paulos also stands apart from the great bulk of both art and illustration, remaining rare and surprising even in the smaller territory of devotional art.

Getting personal

It is impossible to write this brief history of papercutting, knowing that it will appear in this book, *In the Midst of Chaos, Peace*, without confessing a personal acquaintance with the artists and a tremendous respect for both of them and for their work. However, without the slightest fear of sincere contradiction, I can safely say that my great appreciation of the work in this book does not stem from my familiarity with the artists. On the contrary, I became familiar with the artists and even learned to love them both because I was already in awe of their skills as devotional artists. I am not a Catholic, and yet nearly every image produced by either of these artists is able to inspire in me the very feelings I believe they represent in the artists.

Where do Sister Mary Jean and Dan stand in the history of papercutting? Having surveyed the terrain of cut-paper art produced over the past centuries, even over more than two thousand years, I have to conclude that these artists are securely and properly positioned as contemporary masters of the cut-paper form in devotional art. Even apart from the strictures of the devotional, they both achieve, with the seeming simplicity of illustration, effects that are correctly seen as achievements of fine art.

From at least as far back as the *Klosterarbeit* of the late Middle Ages and the Renaissance to the present, the tradition of cut-paper Madonnas and saints is unbroken. I believe that the images in this book are among the finest and most moving ever produced. In an age of photography and image manipulation, in an art-world atmosphere of shock values and repetitive illustration, Sister Mary Jean and Dan have rejected all that is easy and common and have stretched themselves instead toward what is rare and inspiring, and perhaps also inspired.

If there is a mistake that a viewer might make when looking at papercuttings in general and those in this book particularly, it is this: He might be moved to think that "it's only cut-paper" and that there is little to see. This would be a grave mistake, especially when the examples of the art form are as fine as the ones in this book, balancing almost magically their adherence to ancient tradition and the visionary innovations of the artists.

JOSEPH W. BEAN
Writer, artist, historian

You are not a saint because you keep the rules and are blameless; you are a saint if you live in the real world, going out and loving the real people whom God has put into your life.

Beneath all grief, the most fundamental of realities is joy itself. It is never our own, never within our power. Rather, we are taken up into its vastness, and what we experience is not true joy, but its residue: our reactions, our emotions, after the vision has left us. Often joy establishes us so securely in itself, and in the remembrance of its presence, that we can quite comfortably cope with whatever life has to throw at us.

God does not intervene to change the circumstances of our life: what He does do, with the most compassionate faithfulness, is enable us to make those circumstances fruitful. Death remains death, but it is also a new life: pain accepted from His hands purifies, transforms, redeems. God is what happens to us; His presence makes everything potential for growth in love and goodness. Yes, let Him make us holy.

The center of our beautiful religion is Jesus. He is the only Man Who has looked into the cloud, seen with His own eyes the Face of the holy mystery, and turned round to assure us that the name of God is "Father".

QUEEN OF THE UNIVERSE

No understanding of God is real if we do not use the means we have at hand, and spiritual reading is one of them. But it must not be arid reading, feeding the mind alone. The great significance of meditation is not that it urges us to mortification, but that it makes clear that life and death are full of suffering, and that there is no easy way to live or die.

CHRISTMAS ROSE

The blessing of peace is in knowing that we have only to do what we morally can, and then live without repining in the outcome. Those we love die; possessions are stolen or diminished; only goodness remains. Yet, however terrible our suffering, it will not last forever. On that condition is based our peace.

Before the cross, Jesus endured the constraints of the earth. Having given up to the uttermost His own will, He was able to go where nature could not take Him. Suffering and death are never intended as destructions, as obstacles to fullness of being. They become so, all too often, because we refuse to give up our will and to seek in the pain the divine meaning. Jesus absolutely trusted His Father, understanding that the agony was life-giving.

Love must be able to say "No" as well as "Yes" and even to seem unloving if, in the end, that is for the other's betterment.

So often while we look at sacred images we feel so small, perhaps even insignificant. Yet, other times we can feel great because, looking at them, we magnify our own selves.

Joseph was the one who had to leave the safety of the family to earn their bread, the one whose task demanded that he be absent for much of the day from the loving presence of his family. Joseph appeared, often, to be an outsider, but through vocation, not choice. He always "performed his humble role" with gentle dignity. The love which consumed him was not to be found in expressions of long periods of intimacy with his beloved, but in doing what best served their needs. Joseph put God first, and himself nowhere. The cost? A low-key but totally redemptive death-to-self.

Entering into silence should be like stepping into cool, clear water. The dust and debris are quietly washed away and we are purified of our triviality. We are simplified, beautified, and should be mindful that we have only to be still, letting God's grace refresh us and the sunlight of His peace shine upon us.

Christ, though divine, was also human as we are, and He knew weakness. But He could cling in His weakness and sorrow to His Father, with an absolute sureness, whatever He may have felt or endured. "Though He slay me, yet will I trust in Him."

Most people can manage to be cheerful enough, but this, however admirable, has nothing to do with joy. Joy is a liberating power, an absolute gift. And though it is not won or deserved, it is often the resource which transforms our times of despair and horror. Joy is the victory over our struggles.

Aluigi Gonzaga

From the very start of our religion, the saints, weak and imperfect, like ourselves, simply said a total "Yes" to God's love. It is not that they were strong enough or virtuous enough to win His love, because that love is always freely given, but only those we call saints actually did that "blessed taking", accepting the reality of being loved with all its consequences. God's definition is simply "love", and the saints surrendered to its meaning.

God will not transform us if we insist on offering Him only our goodness, our successes, our strengths. Controlled prayer is only partial prayer: it is the giving up of the control to God that makes prayer true.

QUEEN OF ROSES

There is a certain satisfaction in thinking ill of ourselves, both in that it confirms us in a hope of our lack of conceit and in that it flatters our laziness. A gift always means *we* have to work with it and so *we* may prefer not to be overtly aware of our own potential. So pray! God sees us in our absolute truth, and seeing us, just as *we are*, He loves us and brings us to blissful fulfillment.

Peace is a deliberate choice. It needs no external support; therefore we find in its blessing an immense freedom. Peace is a passionate commitment to becoming a full person.

It is pure giving when something is given in secret because we are alerted to another's needs, not asking a single thing in return—other than making someone happy!

GARDEN OF THE ETERNAL FATHER

To give those we love their independence, to accept that we cannot make their choices for them, that they cannot live by our hard-earned experience—this is part of love! We have to allow those we love to "choose their own butterflies". For some, the chase will be ever elusive, and love must work within that painful understanding.

When the crucifixion is described by an artist, it comes very close to the bone for me, because it shows the death of someone I love. The art takes us beyond what some people would consider as the "narrowness of religion" by making it so clear that a religion only works when it is based upon the deepest experiences of the human heart.

What matters is not silence itself, which can be merely physical, but what we do within it. The great mystic Teresa of Avila called the mind a "clacking mill". We can, indeed, still the mind through intense psychic application, but such application—directed wholly to the self—may be so self-satisfying as to abnegate its very purpose. The purpose of silence is directed stillness, which receives rather than acts. There is only one state of perfect freedom from "clacking" thoughts— and that is ecstasy. Ecstasy is pure gift and not for our seeking. As soon as we seek, self comes in and renders such efforts useless!

Reverence is the heart's deepest form of respect, of love. It accepts that we as individuals are not essential to the universe.

Jesus was drained, bloodless for our sake. We are confronted each time we see a crucifix with the kenosis of the Savior. We must choose to stand up and compassionate Him, seeking to understand the true meaning of this self-emptying.

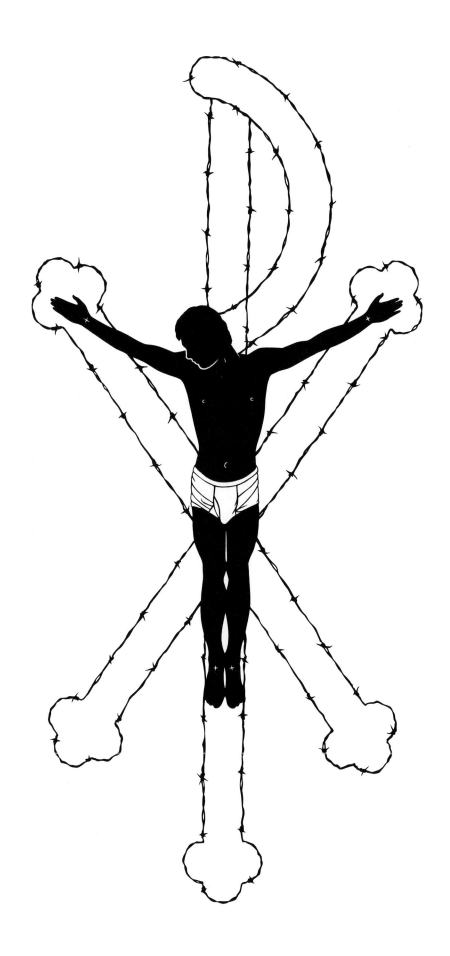

Gazing upon sacred art is an exercise in prayer! The artists, by their very nature, and perhaps without even knowing it, teach us to pray!

AE CAME ALL SO STILL

There is no saint who did not, who does not long for wisdom, and she is always there in answer to our prayer. To be a saint is a wholly practical and realistic growth into our own truth.

The path to peace is not to seek it, but to seek selflessness. Self-seeking of any kind narrows our potential and destroys the balance on which peace depends. Peace is one of our deepest needs. Too often we misunderstand the nature of it. We should not try to control our lives. If we are set upon doing so, we have abdicated from peace.

The instruments of the cross became the flight of Jesus' freedom. He was drained, bloodless for our sake. His blood and pain, the nails, the cross—all have been transformed into the glory of ascension.

Love, in itself, is a blessing! True love cannot be extinguished or diminished. Whatever changes in the loved one, true love stays firm. It will deepen but not lessen. To love simply means to put others before ourselves, to rise above the pettiness of ego, and in doing that, we can never go amiss.

Mary, Incense of Sweetness, Pray for us to Our Lord, Your Son.

Sometimes it takes silence to shake our lives into perspective. Yes, in silence we can actually break the hold time has on us, and accept that our true home is not here on earth, but in eternity.

It is a tragedy that for many people the center of Christmas seems to be a commercial idea of Santa Claus. They forget completely that *we* are celebrating the birth of Christ, that Jesus and Mary are the meaning of Christmas. But if we know who Santa Claus is: that he is the generous, sweet, sensitive Saint Nicholas who loved to give things to people in need, perhaps *we* can go through the present-giving and the merrymaking to the true meaning: the birth of our Redeemer.

Prayer is based wholly on being truthful. If we want God to be our all, then we shall want to do whatever pleases Him. Prayer is the only human action or state where cheating is impossible.

There is wisdom in knowing what is inevitable and what, with courage and intelligence, can be changed. Fundamentally though, nothing matters except to have a true and humble desire to do what we know is right.

Pain, like joy, can be turned selfishly inward and tie us up with ego-concern. It is meant to teach us trust, to open our hearts to the reality of God, to be redemptive, as it was for Our Lord. The grace to turn bitterness into sweetness and let suffering make us holy comes from prayer and the sacraments. At worship, our prayers are united with those of Jesus, and this marvellous act of unification will energize our day.

True Devotion to Mary began with Jesus

None of us can claim a perfect record in love. We all fail and betray, even inadvertently. This is perhaps the worst pain of love, failure for which we feel culpable. Yet, what all love knows is repentance for inadequacy.

The taking of Christ was a violent scene. Only a willing surrender to love can truly "take" us, and those who come to "take" are unwitting instruments of that love. Judas "took" Jesus to the death that offered not only his own redemption but ours as well.

Mary's life was a life of loneliness and poverty, with her Son dying a criminal's death. Her only solace was faith!

Profound silence is not something we fall into casually. This may indeed happen, and a blessed happening it is, but normally we choose to set aside a time and a place to enter into spiritual quietness. Thus, silence is essentially a surrender to the holiness of the Divine Mystery.

If one is going to spend hours praying every day, these cannot be hours of talking, or asking, but hours of loving. Prayer is essentially resting one's head on the heart of God, certain that He knows our every need. Yes, prayer is complete surrender!

Prayer is God's taking possession of us. We expose to Him what we are, and He gazes on us with the creative eye of Holy Love. His gaze is transforming: He does not leave us in our poverty but draws into being all we are meant to become.

98

There is power in a very name. Even pagans know this. To know someone's name means to have power over him, however external: he will, after all, turn around if you name him aloud, stop in his tracks, look up. Imagine the power in the Name of Jesus! Think of the Holy Name! It will hold us back during times of temptation, just long enough for sanity to take over. Jesus. Jesus. Jesus. Often call upon Him!

Perfect love is practiced rather than written out. It makes no demands and seeks nothing for itself. Jesus shows us that perfect love is unconditional; for it to be love at all, the other's happiness always comes first.

When the angel came from heaven to ask a creature of earth if she would become the Mother of God, Mary was just a child, who had hardly bosomed at all—there was just a gentle curve to be seen. This was a very fraught moment. Mary patiently awaited the completion of the angel's message so that she could eagerly obey.

All love, whether of child, parent, friend, even of place, possession, or animal, holds the potential for suffering, because of death. We cannot possess or hold fast anything or anyone: it is all gift. Life contains inevitable partings and inescapable pain. The loveless are protected against this suffering: the zombie feels nothing at all! We are alive in proportion to our response to love, and our pain at parting is in proportion to the extent of that love.

During His death on the cross, Jesus made no overt appeals to us; He concentrated upon His prayer, that innermost secret, the very essence of His soul, still hidden and mysterious in our own prayer. Yet, we learned the meaning of what faith puts before us. We either offer our own hearts to receive the prayer of Jesus, or we refuse.

BENEDICTUS
FRUCTUS
VENTRIS
TUI

The noises of the world, in thoughts or activities, drown out the silent sounds of heavenly graces that come to all of us, one way or another.

In each of us, there should be a union between the decision-making part, with its passion and energy, and the loving, quiet part of us. It is the wise and gentle part that keeps the active, choosing part from making wrong decisions.

Christ is Wisdom Incarnate, and unless we share in this holy wisdom, we can be shamefully weak in what we call "love".

To express what one means, and to hear what another says—this is a rare thing!

If we do not know God, how can we love Him? Ignorant love is false. Love craves to know, to understand, to enter into the mood of the Beloved. With God, the process is almost terrible in its simplicity. We know the Lord through using our minds: reading, meditating, asking questions. We know Him from our hearts: praying, surrendering, keeping silence. Wanting God is the essential prerequisite.

Through the surrendering to His Passion we understand the integral meaning of Jesus. He waited in patience for His deliverance, not FROM disaster, but THROUGH it. In Him, we too are free when entrapped, empowered to make all our distress a holy purification.

Mary summons us, not with her eyes, nor even with her voice, but always with her hands, empty, telling us how empty our life is without the fulfillment of the loved one, the other part of her own being. Her constant, silent summons is a sublime invitation to become a full human being.

Sanctity means recognizing the whole of us, the generic flaws that God's grace must purify and the genetic virtues that grace must also infuse, in case we rely on their natural power. We must not sweep a single part of ourselves under the carpet! God knows exactly what we are like, good and bad, and how much of it is our "fault".

Christ's Passion overcame death, drawing life out of darkness and wringing hope out of despair. In the purity of this beauty alone, sacred art celebrates eternity, which is what it is all about.

INDEX OF ILLUSTRATIONS

This list provides the page numbers, titles, and sizes of the cuttings; the year they were executed; and, in italics, the owners of the originals. In most cases, Sister Mary Jean Dorcy did not keep records of her cuttings. Hence, only where the information was recorded in her own writing is it listed below.